Come to Central Park

Chanit Roston, Paintings   **Pamela King, Text**

Text and paintings copyright 2012 and 2015
By Chanit Roston and Pamela King

First Edition

Published by
Green Trees and Blue Skies Publishing Co., Inc.
689 Ft. Washington Avenue, 4G
New York, New York 10040

ISBN 978-1-5136-0242-4

www.cometocentralpark.com

www.chanit.com

**Hi, I am Max. I live in Central Park in New York City.
Let me introduce you to the park and my friends who live here, too.**

At night, Skydancer, one of my best friends, gallops among the stars.

He told me that the Earth spins 'round and 'round just like the carousel.

My friend, Balto, a courageous Siberian Huskie, raced his dogsled through a heavy snowstorm and saved the children in Nome, Alaska.

Even though he is a hero, he does not talk about it much.

I often visit Alice in Wonderland. She is curious.

She wonders about everything.

It is always fun to row around the lake.

Time stops when the oars are lifted.

My very best friend is the Angel Bethesda. I love her.

I tell her my secrets and she never tells anyone.

Occasionally, I visit the boat pond where children launch their little boats.

As the wind catches the sails, the boats tack and race across the water.

From time to time, I walk across the Bow Bridge and look at the skyline.

Central Park is a green oasis amidst canyons of concrete, glass and steel.

Hans Christian Andersen's stories teach us how to be kind.

Many children love to come and hear, "Once upon a time . . . ."

**When I visit Belvedere Castle, the weather station in Central Park,
I like to make believe that I am royalty at the castle.**

I am happy being who I am.
Yet sometimes I enjoy imagining that I am someone else.

I care about my animal friends at the zoo. The red panda likes to snooze in the sunshine, and the mischievous seals are always amusing.

I would like to befriend the penguins. They seem so cool.

At the skating rink, people put on their skates to the sound of the music.

They get their balance and start spinning and gliding across the ice.

Everyone loves sledding fast down Dog Hill.

**Huffing and puffing,
you have to pull the sled up so you can fly down again and again!**

There are signs in the park saying not to feed us.

Never, ever feed the wildlife. It is against the rules.

Everything you do in Central Park is fun.
You can walk or stroll, climb boulders, ride a bike, or lie in the grass.

It is a wonderful place to feel free.

Dear Readers,

   This is a book that lets you enter the paintings and be in Central Park. While you are visiting, you can talk with your child about the laws of nature and gravity and about how the Earth spins 'round and 'round just like the carousel. You can discuss what it means to be a hero and not talk about it, or what it means to be humble and not boast. One line, "Time stops when the oars are lifted," can lead to a discussion about stopping, slowing down and noticing the world. Just stop and look and see! If we look and see we become curious like Alice in Wonderland, and our curiosity leads to new understandings and new discoveries! And, of course, everyone needs someone to tell a secret to. Secrets can be our dreams and goals and what we know inside. Maybe the child doesn't know what "tacking" is and so that can lead to a great lesson in geometry. And the line "Central Park is a green oasis . . ." may be a wonderful first introduction to metaphor. All the attributes of an oasis, it is refreshing and a source of life, are applied to Central Park, and the child learns how we use one thing to help us understand another. Hans Christian Andersen's stories teach children to be kind because those stories, like fairytales in general, have kindness as an essential theme. When there are three brothers in a story, it is always the kind brother in the tale who wins out in the end! We all know that children love to be actors, play dress up, and pretend they are someone else. This helps them imagine who they want to be. When we learn to skate we have to learn to have balance, and balance is a skill that we can always use. Keep your balance all your life! What a great seed to sow. The idea of balance can also lead to a discussion of justice and fair play. Children really want things to be fair! To keep having fun and going down the hill, you have to work hard and pull the sled back up. Work and fun can go together which calls for another kind of balance. And, without a doubt, we have to learn there are rules in the world (don't feed the wildlife), which we should adhere to. Life has rules. Human food just isn't good for the animals. Then at the end, we read that Central Park is a wonderful place to feel free. If we can feel free, we can be happy! Being joyful can be a wonderful goal in life. Maybe it is the essence of everything. We hope the grownup reader does more with these simple words than just read them. We call our book an "Interactive Reader," and we invite readers and listeners to actively interact and have discussions about life. Finally, you may wonder where Max is. Perhaps you can see his shadow or imagine where he is hiding. We hope the paintings are doorways to the Imagination. Enjoy!

                     Chanit and Pamela

About the Authors

Chanit Roston

Pamela King

Chanit Roston and Pamela King have been friends forever. They met shortly after they arrived in New York in the 1960s, and from the first time they went to Central Park, they fell in love with it. They have always thought of Central Park as the "heart" of the city. Once their children were born, their pleasure was magnified as each rock and stone, grate and tunnel, nook and cranny was explored and found delightful.

Chanit studied drawing with Joseph Hirsh and painting with Harvey Dinnerstein at the National Academy of Fine Art and Design, with Robert Phillip at the Art Students League and was privately mentored by Anthony Toney. Chanit's paintings have been shown at galleries such as the National Academy of Fine art and Design in New York City and the Guild Hall Museum in East Hampton. A show of her diverse work was also exhibited at the Asman Gallery (NBC News Building) in Washington, D.C. You can see her portraits of "People, Places and Things" at her website, www.chanit.com.

Pamela has been a New York City high school ESL and English teacher for the past 20 years. She received her doctorate from Teachers College, Columbia University in 2011 where she studied metaphoric errors second language learners make as they learn English. She adores the English language and helping her students succeed in their new lives in America.

Chanit's love of the visual and Pamela's love for words, as well as their shared love for Central Park, has led to *Come to Central Park*. For them it is a magical place for joy, rejuvenation and just plain fun. If you don't know it yet, they hope you, too, will fall in love with Central Park, and if it's one of your favorite places, as well, they hope that this book will give you renewed delight as you read it and share it with the ones you love.